IMPROMPTU ON NUNS' ISLAND

Michel Tremblay

Translated by Linda Gaboriau

Talonbooks
2002

Talonbooks
P.O. Box 2076, Vancouver, British Columbia, Canada V6B 3S3
www.talonbooks.com

Typeset in New Baskerville and printed and bound in Canada.

First Printing: September 2002

L'État des lieux was published in the original French by Leméac Édieur,
Montréal, Québec in 2002.

National Library of Canada Cataloguing in Publication Data
Tremblay, Michel, 1942-
 [État des lieux. English]
 Impromptu on Nuns' Island

 A play.
 Translation of: L'état des lieux.
 ISBN 0-88922-470-6

 I. Gaboriau, Linda. II. Title.
 PS8539.R47E8213 2002   C842'.54   C2002-910843-8
 PQ3919.2.T73E8213 2002

The publisher gratefully acknowledges the financial support of the
Canada Council for the Arts; the Government of Canada through the
Book Publishing Industry Development Program; and the Province of
British Columbia through the British Columbia Arts Council for our
publishing activities.

For my friends at l'Agence Goodwin: Camille Goodwin, Marie-Claude Goodwin, Nathalie Goodwin, Louise Jokisch, Dominique Poirer, Johanne Cadotte, Isabelle Lépine, Véronyque Roy, Danielle Lanthier, Hugo Couturier, Jean Chapdelaine and Patrick Leimgruber, who've been taking care of me and protecting me for years. And God knows I need it!

L'État des lieux was first performed at Théâtre du Nouveau Monde, Montreal, on April 23, 2002, with the following cast:

ESTELLE . . . . Rita Lafontaine
PATRICIA . . . . Marthe Turgeon
MICHELLE . . . . Kathleen Fortin
RICHARD . . . . Denis Paris
Directed by André Brassard
Set design by Danièle Lévesque
Costume design by François Laplante
Lighting design by Michel Beaulieu
Music by Larsen Lupin
Assistant Director and Stage Manager: Jean Bélanger

The first English-language production of *Impromptu on Nuns' Island* was co-produced by Centaur Theatre Company, Montreal and Tarragon Theatre, Toronto. Its premiere presentation took place on October 24, 2002 at Centaur Theatre under the artistic direction of Gordon McCall, with the following cast:

ESTELLE . . . . Patricia Hamilton
PATRICIA . . . . Dixie Seatle
MICHELLE . . . . Diana Donnelly
RICHARD . . . . Robert Persichini
Directed by Diana Leblanc
Set design by Guido Tondino
Costume design by Victoria Zimski
Lighting design by Steven Hawkins
Assistant Director: Graham Cozzubbo
Stage Manager: Wendy Rockburn

Translator's Note

For the benefit of readers who might wish to compare this translation with the original as published by Leméac Éditeur, it is important to note that, at the playwrights request, the translation is based on the script as it was revised for the original production at Théâtre du Nouveau Monde in Montreal.

Characters

ESTELLE (late sixties)
PATRICIA (late forties)
MICHELLE (late twenties)
RICHARD (early forties)

The three women are reunited briefly in Patricia's penthouse apartment on Nuns' Island. They are joined by Richard, who, at the beginning and the end, is in a world and a setting of his own.

*The Salomé theme from Richard Strauss' Salomé is
heard, twice.*

Then Herod shouts:

VOICE OF HEROD:
Man töte dieses Weib!

*Herod's guards crush Salomé beneath their shields.
RICHARD is sitting on a piano bench facing the
audience.*

He only occasionally glances at the keyboard.

Under the piano, a huge duffel bag.

RICHARD:
It's funny ... I asked for this special appointment, but
everything I'm about to tell you is already very clear.
I mean ... I repeated it to myself during the seven
and a half hours I just spent on the flight back from
Paris, I went over it a hundred times in my head, the
way you relive a recital ... I'm not saying I prepared a
little number for you, that's not it, but, almost ...
Suddenly, everything seemed so clear, at one point I
even thought, maybe I don't need you anymore, if I
understand my problem so well, maybe I can work it
out on my own. But just repeating it over and over in
my head wasn't enough ... I had to hear myself say it
out loud, to someone else, someone who'd listen to
me, someone whose job it is to listen to me ... and
find me interesting! Even though I'm not so sure you
find me interesting ... Do you find your clients interesting? Actually, I haven't been seeing you long
enough for you to find me interesting ... During the
four or five sessions we had before I left, I didn't
really open up, I told you superficial stuff, I beat

7

around the bush, I watched you watch me without saying a thing, with your poker face, as if nothing I said had any effect on you … You looked straight at me, but I couldn't read anything in your eyes … like right now. I talked and talked, because talking comes easy to me, everyone complains about that, but I guess I wasn't ready to face my real problem, so I talked about any old thing. You must've realized that, you must be used to it. I don't know if some people arrive ready to confide in you, on the spot … Probably not, if they need to see a psychologist. So now, because I'm ready to face my problem, because I think I understand what's been making me feel so unhappy, so ashamed of myself for so long, I feel as if I've understood everything and solved the whole thing. At least, that's how it feels … I feel lighter because I put my finger on it all by myself, but stupid because it took me so long … even though I know that I knew all along, but I just didn't want to *see* it! *(silence)* So, in a nutshell, to cut a long story short, my problem is … I'm a famous diva's pet poodle!

PATRICIA enters her apartment, followed by her daughter MICHELLE.

She drops her carry-on bag in the middle of the room, while MICHELLE sets down the two suitcases she was carrying.

PATRICIA:
Phew, feels good to speak my own language! I haven't spoken Québécois for months! After speaking prissy Parisian in France, and all over Europe, by the end of every day, I'd get cramps around my mouth!

MICHELLE:
Honestly, Ma!

PATRICIA:

It's true! When they say the French use muscles around the mouth that we never use, it's absolutely true! I'm the living proof of it. I'd get back to my hotel room at night, and I'd have to massage the corners of my mouth, like this ... It hurt so much!

MICHELLE:

Good thing you never exaggerate!

PATRICIA:

It's true! To say nothing of my sore throat! *(in a phoney accent)* No kidding, my throat was on fire, from rolling my r's. Whenever the interviews were too long, towards the end, I'd start making faces, the interviewers must've thought I had nervous tics!

MICHELLE laughs.

MICHELLE:

You'll never change ...

PATRICIA:

No way ... it's too late for that. At the opera house in Munich last month, while we were rehearsing *Rosenkavalier*, a terrible flop, by the way, a hor-rendous production, I came out with a few juicy Québécois swear words. Everyone thought it was hilarious and the conductor kept saying: "Say something to me in French Canadian, Patsy!" He should have paid less attention to my French Canadian accent, and more attention to his music. Dutoit never asked me to use my Québécois accent, on the contrary! Anyway! Where's your grandmother?

MICHELLE:

She's probably busy insulting some taxi cab driver, as usual ... They're all still terrified of her, you know ...

9

PATRICIA:

Watch what you say, Michelle ... *(with a smile)* It's a sickness—

MICHELLE:

(laughing) It's not a sickness, she's just plain unpleasant, period.

PATRICIA:

Still as bad as ever?

MICHELLE:

Worse than ever ... Apparently she's become a living legend among the cab drivers. When the dispatcher gives her address, they all call in sick!

PATRICIA:

She'll get over it. *(looking at herself in a mirror)* Gawd, it's good to be home! You didn't get the living room repainted, like I asked you?

MICHELLE:

Ma, you asked me last week!

PATRICIA:

It was longer ago than that!

MICHELLE:

Let's say two weeks ago ...

PATRICIA:

I've always hated that café au lait.

MICHELLE:

You're the one who wanted it, you nagged for weeks!

PATRICIA:

Well, I don't want it anymore.

MICHELLE:

You'd seen it somewhere ... at Patrick Dupont's, I think—

PATRICIA:

Patrick Dupont always had lousy taste.

MICHELLE:
That's not what you said then—

PATRICIA:
Forget what I said then, and have it done pearl grey,
like I asked you.

MICHELLE:
You wanted apricot pink!

PATRICIA:
I never said that!

MICHELLE:
Ma!

PATRICIA:
Anyway, now I want my living room pearl grey! Don't
I have the right? I'm the one who's paying for it.

MICHELLE:
When you start in on that—

PATRICIA:
Let's not argue, I just arrived ... Look at me ... Have
you gained a couple of pounds?

MICHELLE:
You say that every time you come back—

PATRICIA:
And it's true every time, too!

MICHELLE:
Ma, I'd weigh four hundred pounds!

PATRICIA:
Isn't that what do you weigh? C'mon, I'm just
kidding! Can't you take a joke? I know, you keep
gaining and losing the same ten pounds. And right
now, you're gaining them! *(She hugs her daughter and
gives her a big kiss.)*

PATRICIA:
I'm so happy to see you. How long has it been?

11

MICHELLE:
Almost eight months.

PATRICIA:
No! Has it been that long?

MICHELLE:
Last time you left, it was for the *Turandot* at Covent Garden.

PATRICIA:
God, you're right. Did you read the reviews I faxed you?

MICHELLE:
Of course, and the ones on *Butterfly*, too. And the ones on *Nabucco*, at the Bastille in Paris.

PATRICIA:
They said I looked like an overstuffed sausage in that costume, and they were right. Nobody could sing in it—

MICHELLE:
That's not true, for once, all of your reviews were great—

PATRICIA:
Since when do critics know their ass from their elbow … Don't read that stuff …

MICHELLE:
So why do you send them to me?

PATRICIA:
(ignoring the question) That role is impossible to sing to begin with. And that costume was so tight, I told Thomas Hampson who was singing Nabucco to tear it off me if he saw me turn purple! And that's no exaggeration!

MICHELLE can't help but smile.

MICHELLE:
Is he as handsome as ever?

PATRICIA:
   What? Who?

MICHELLE:
   Thomas Hampson. You were all gaga over him a few
   years ago.

PATRICIA:
   Was I?

MICHELLE:
   So ... is there someone else on the scene now?

PATRICIA:
   Have you ever heard of a baritone named Simon
   Keenlyside?

MICHELLE:
   Well, well, that one's got staying power. You were
   talking about him last year.

RICHARD:
   I thought I'd have more of an effect! I delivered my
   punch line five minutes ago, and you haven't batted
   an eyelash. Seems intriguing to me, someone who
   says he's someone else's pet poodle! I expected, I
   don't know, a raising of the eyebrow, a glimmer of
   interest in the back of your eyes, I thought you might
   lean forward a bit, rest your elbows on your desk, or
   something ...

PATRICIA:
   (glancing at her watch) That woman has spent her
   entire life being late.

MICHELLE:
   She's not late, Ma, she's making us wait.

RICHARD:
   If I told you that woman is Patricia Pasquetti, alias,
   Patricia Paquette, Patsy to her friends, of which she
   has many, would you find it a bit more exciting?

PATRICIA:
She has to be the only person on earth who dares make me wait.

RICHARD:
I guess not. Well, I'll just pretend I'm talking to a brick wall.

MICHELLE:
We wait for you, often enough. All the time. Everywhere.

PATRICIA:
Have you ever met a star who wasn't late? But I suppose I'm the only star you know.

MICHELLE:
So ... You missed the language, but your old contempt sure comes back fast.

PATRICIA:
It's not contempt.

MICHELLE:
Then what is it?

PATRICIA:
A simple observation. You can't be a real star in a town like Montreal, face it!

MICHELLE:
A hole like Montreal, you mean.

Her mother looks at her, but doesn't answer.

MICHELLE:
Some looks say more than a thousand words, right?

RICHARD:
I'm her accompanist on the piano. Patricia Pasquetti's. When she needs me, no matter where she is in the world, all she has to do is pick up the phone ... and to use the same image, I come running like her puppy dog! For an evening of Schubert, or Schumann, or Richard Strauss. And afterwards, I

pack my little suitcase and head home. And I wait for her next call. Oh, I have a profession ... I earn my living as an accompanist at the Music Conservatory, and at McGill ... But when Madame needs me, I come running.

PATRICIA:
A critic once said about me that even if there were no words to the operas I sing, people would understand the story—because of the look in my eyes.

MICHELLE:
C'mon, how dumb can you get?

PATRICIA:
I thought it was rather nice, myself ...

MICHELLE:
Nice, but dumb! Must've been one of those sissy, opera-loving Frenchmen, as you always say.

PATRICIA:
You're talking about my audience!

MICHELLE:
You're the one who refers to them like that.

PATRICIA:
Not anymore ...

MICHELLE:
No, not since one of them heard you, and didn't know what the Québécois expression meant.

PATRICIA:
(laughing) So I told you that one?

MICHELLE:
Yeah! That call must've cost you a fortune, we laughed for so long!

PATRICIA:
You have to admit it was funny. How did I answer him again?

MICHELLE:

> *(with a prissy accent)* What does that word mean? You
> don't know what it means? Well, my friend, it ... it
> means ... a fag, there, is that clear?
>
> *They laugh.*

PATRICIA:

> You should've seen the look on his face! He had
> these little stick-out ears, and they turned so red, they
> could've lit up the whole cocktail party.
>
> *They laugh some more.*

RICHARD:

> Do you know how I chose you? It's important for the
> rest of the story ... I was looking for a psychologist ...
> who knew something about music. I didn't know if
> there was such a thing, but I asked around. Then one
> day, this woman I know mentioned you. She'd heard
> about a psychologist who had a grand piano in his
> office. I couldn't believe it. She even said that
> sometimes, between appointments, people heard him
> play. Classical music. I liked the idea that you played
> piano between your appointments, instead of resting.
> And that's why I decided to come see you ...
>
> *He stands up abruptly.*

RICHARD:

> Please, do something, anything, to let me know
> you're listening to me. I feel as if I'm talking to
> someone who's deaf and dumb. *(silence)* Good, thank
> you.
>
> *He sits down again.*

MICHELLE:

> I'm sorry I couldn't pick you up at the airport. But,
> like I told you on the phone, it was an important
> rehearsal.

PATRICIA:

I remember your saying you could hire substitutes for television rehearsals ... *(a bit contemptuously)* Pay someone to take notes for you, or something ...

MICHELLE:

I don't like doing that. I don't think it's professional. Showing up at the taping with somebody else's notes doesn't seem fair to my colleagues. Besides, I like rehearsing.

PATRICIA:

C'mon, if your colleagues do it ...

MICHELLE:

That's their business. I don't work that way.

PATRICIA:

Well, that's how you end up letting people walk all over you, my dear.

MICHELLE:

Don't start in on that again, please!

PATRICIA:

(changing the subject) How do you think I felt when the doors to customs slid open and there was no one there to greet me? I looked like a nobody. I signed a couple of autographs, and pretended I was looking for someone. One man even offered to share a taxi with me! Do you believe it!

MICHELLE:

Sorry! I didn't have time to alert the journalists. But I found the time to send a limousine, didn't I?

PATRICIA:

Thank god, otherwise I would've died of embarrassment.

MICHELLE:

Anyway, it's obvious I couldn't have gone to pick you up, we arrived downstairs at the same time. And I

17

can't see you waiting at the airport for an hour with your fleet of red suitcases.

PATRICIA:

By the way, who's paying for that limousine?

MICHELLE:

I am, Ma! I am. Instead of paying for a substitute, I paid for your limousine.

PATRICIA:

(sharply) I hope it wasn't more expensive!

MICHELLE:

I can afford to pay for your limousine, Ma ...

PATRICIA:

It's about time!

MICHELLE:

Maybe it's taken a while, maybe I'm not a world famous opera singer, even if I do have the figure for it, but I finally earn enough money to send a limousine to meet my mother at Dorval Airport!

PATRICIA:

Anyway, that's Montreal for you ... Name me one star from Montreal who is more than a local star!

RICHARD:

But I had to end up with the mutest psychologist in town. You might know music but you sure don't share your knowledge with your clients! Is that your style? You wait until we break down before you let us know you're still breathing? Well, I'm having a breakdown right now! I might not be foaming at the mouth and rolling my eyes, *but I'm having a breakdown!* Because I'm sick of being an asshole.

MICHELLE:

What really happened in Paris?

PATRICIA:

You know how to hurt a girl, don't you?

MICHELLE:
I was well-trained ...

PATRICIA:
Which version did you read? The one in *Le Monde* or the one in *Figaro*?

MICHELLE:
The one in *Le Devoir.*

PATRICIA:
Must've been a reprint of the one in *Le Monde.*

MICHELLE rolls her eyes.

PATRICIA:
It's not the actual incident that upset me, things like that happen to all of us ... Not always at the Paris Opera, fortunately, but still ... Okay, so my voice cracked, I let out a squawk that will go down in the annals of opera, but it wasn't my fault—

MICHELLE:
It was because you were breaking up.

PATRICIA:
That's right. And you can't control that.

RICHARD:
She calls me at the last minute to come save her life, then she treats me like shit.

PATRICIA:
But it's what happened afterwards ... two days later.

RICHARD:
Yes, yes, yes, her, Patricia Pasquetti. The great Paquette!

PATRICIA:
The actual incident ...

RICHARD:
My benefactor ...

PATRICIA:

What can I say, it was funny, hilarious, that's all there is to it …

RICHARD:

… my fairy godmother …

PATRICIA:

… nobody I know could've resisted!

RICHARD:

My patron!

PATRICIA:

Nobody!

RICHARD:

At least, that's how she sees herself …

PATRICIA:

But why me!

RICHARD:

When in fact … she's my tormentor!

PATRICIA:

Maria would've told them to futz off and moved on … But Patricia Paquette wanted to save face!

MICHELLE:

Typical …

PATRICIA:

That's right, dear. Even in the face of adversity, I'm efficient! I could've fallen flat on my face a second time, but fortunately my plan worked … And I've returned triumphant to my home town where they didn't even roll out a straw mat to welcome me!

RICHARD:

You smiled! You actually smiled! I saw you! Do I have to use big words to revive you?

PATRICIA:
They say they're proud of your accomplishments abroad, but when you come back, they treat you like dirt.

MICHELLE:
Who does?

RICHARD:
Well, those words are no exaggeration.

MICHELLE:
The audience?

RICHARD:
I'd even say I'm weighing my words.

PATRICIA:
Of course not. The people who earn a living talking about what you do.

RICHARD:
She calls me at the last minute asking me to come save her life, and when I save her life, she treats me like shit! But I'm repeating myself.

MICHELLE:
"The little people" as you always called them.

PATRICIA:
And "little" is a big word for them.

MICHELLE:
You can't be mad that they didn't bring out the crowds to welcome you—nobody knows you're back!

RICHARD:
But one thing at a time. I'll tell you what happened … before and during my flying visit to Paris, and you can judge for yourself …

PATRICIA:
I know that … but let me fume a bit, it makes me feel better …

RICHARD:

It all began at the Opéra Bastille in Paris, less than a week ago.

PATRICIA:

They all reported that I broke up, but nobody said there was good reason, that it was totally justified!

MICHELLE:

Breaking up on stage is unforgivable, Ma.

PATRICIA:

The only thing that's unforgivable on stage, my dear, is mediocrity.

MICHELLE:

Breaking up is part of mediocrity.

PATRICIA:

Touché. You're your mother's daughter.

RICHARD:

It happened during a performance of Richard Strauss' *Salomé*.

PATRICIA:

You heard, it happened at the end of *Salomé*.

RICHARD:

I wasn't there, but she told me the story so many times in the past two days, I feel like I was ... This is what happened ...

PATRICIA:

To cut a long story short ... Listen, it's very simple, the baritone who was supposed to sing Jokanaan was fat and ugly, with warts all over his face, he had bad breath, and that wasn't the only thing that smelled bad, you get the picture, it was hell. The rehearsals were among the worst in my entire career. And if James Conlon, the conductor, hadn't been there to hold me back, I would've walked, and they would've had to call Myriam Ange-Bell.

MICHELLE:
Ma! Myriam Ange-Bell doesn't sing Salomé !

PATRICIA:
She would've learned it in three hours for a chance
to sing at the Paris opera.

MICHELLE:
(shrugging her shoulders) C'mon!

PATRICIA:
Anyway, on opening night, do you believe it, I find
out that the Russian with the unpronounceable name
... Did I tell you he was Russian? Well, he was ...
Anyway, the Russian's sick, and he's been replaced by
a baritone I adore because he's to die for ...

MICHELLE:
And he's not Russian.

PATRICIA:
No way! He's Danish, his name is as
unpronounceable as the other one's, but I'd happily
devote three hours of my life to learn how, just like
Myriam Ange-Bell for *Salomé*. The problem is ... listen
to this, I want it to be clear ... the problem is they
don't have time, between the Russian's phone call
and the performance, to make a head to match my
handsome Dane for the closing scene, impossible ...

MICHELLE:
I can see what's coming ...

PATRICIA:
That's right ... a classic opera story ...

RICHARD:
At the end, during one of the most difficult passages
in the entire opera repertory, they bring Salomé John
the Baptist's head on a platter ...

PATRICIA:

So there I am, you know, in fine form, it's a great show, the Dane was sexy as hell, he sang like a god, I almost felt bad about demanding his head ... Anyway, I do, after performing the most successful dance of the seven veils in my entire career ... and they bring me the wart-covered face of the fat Russian with bad breath! It's stupid, I should've realized, I admit ... but I wasn't prepared for it! James saw something was wrong immediately, because he knows I never hesitate, and he saw me jump and put my hand over my mouth ... as if I'd forgotten my lines! A real amateur! Don't forget I'm supposed to finish that opera in ecstasy, kissing Jokanaan's head on the lips! Breaking up during an opera is the worst thing that can happen! You can't count on your partners, you have notes *you* have to *sing*, a precise beat to follow, *nobody* can help you!

RICHARD:

Imagine! Alone in the middle of the stage at the Opéra Bastille with an uncontrollable case of the giggles!

PATRICIA:

But I managed to hold it together till the end. Then after the famous kiss ... believe me, kissing the lips of a rubber mask that tastes like hell, like glue and dye and the nylon wig, it's bad enough ... and get this, the director *wanted to see my tongue!* Anyway ... when I got to the end, when I'm supposed to sing: "I've kissed you at last, Jokanaan," I ... I don't know ... I lost it, I guess ...

MICHELLE:

And: squawk!

PATRICIA:

A real beauty, too! Not a little blip you can try to disguise as the capriccio of a soprano who finds the emotion, the character's pain, as powerful as the music … oh, no, no, a big squawk, a real beauty, a real contest winner! Just seconds before the end of the show!

RICHARD:
I don't know if you realize what that means for an artist like Madame Pasquetti.

PATRICIA:
I'm not saying it was like Maria's famous false note at the Garnier Opera in the fifties, my fans might be fairies but they're not fools … It hardly affected the applause, the triumph was just a bit less hysterical than usual … maybe one or two curtain calls less … but I knew … and I knew that they knew … my fans who had travelled from far and wide to see me French-kiss a muppet head, and the others, too, the real connoisseurs, the real opera lovers who had just seen me make a fool of myself.

RICHARD:
Can you imagine the disgrace …

PATRICIA:
If you knew what a disgrace—

MICHELLE:
I can imagine, Ma—

PATRICIA:
No, you can't. I wasn't at the Quat'Sous facing a bunch of Montreal nobodies and the two-bit journalists from the local gossip columns! I was at Opera Bastille, facing a squadron of the bitchiest critics in the world! They'll be talking about it for months, for years! It was less than a week ago. Wait till the weeklies come out, and the monthlies, they're the worst! I'll be the laughing stock of opera fans for years to come: "Have you heard the one about Patricia Pasquetti, the Canadian who choked after

tongue-wrestling Jokanaan's head?" I know those people, I've been one of the them since I was a kid.

RICHARD:

A mistake like that in the opera world can be fatal.

PATRICIA:

You know it can be fatal ...

Silence.

MICHELLE lowers her head.

PATRICIA:

And that's just the beginning of the story ... Just the public part that everyone will hear about.

RICHARD:

I had to tell you the whole story so you'll understand what happened afterwards, the part that involves me directly ...

MICHELLE:

Don't tell me they fired you?

PATRICIA:

Oh, they're more ... subtle than that. After the bows, the director threw his arms around me, saying it was barely noticeable. James practically swore that nobody noticed ... but that didn't prevent the newspapers from talking about nothing else the following morning. It wasn't really mean, it was more ... I don't know ... it was more *twisted* than that.

MICHELLE:

You should be glad, you always say that journalists are mean and cruel ... if they spared you, that's great, isn't it?

PATRICIA:

Shh! Do you mind if I finish my story without being interrupted? Thank you.

RICHARD:

When I heard about it on the radio the following morning I thought I'd die of embarrassment for her.

PATRICIA:

False notes happen to everyone, some are more explicable than others, some are more excusable than others ...

MICHELLE:

You don't have to make excuses to me, Ma, I understand—

PATRICIA:

I'm not making excuses! I'm simply explaining what happened! To you, to myself, in my own language! For days now, I've been talking about it and about what happened afterwards, choosing my words, rolling my r's, puckering up my mouth and simpering, like I was born with a particle in front of my name, when I really wanted to swear like a trooper, just like your grandmother when she's too tired to restrain or contain herself! Just wait, she'll probably walk in and let loose with her usual stream of bitchiness, and you know what? ... I'll envy her, because that's exactly what I need to do—just swear my head off from now till the cows come home!

MICHELLE:

Go ahead! Who's stopping you?!

PATRICIA stares at her daughter for a long time before answering.

PATRICIA:

Over there, manners held me back ... here ... it's decency.

MICHELLE:

Decency?

PATRICIA:

That's right, it still exists, you know!

MICHELLE:
It's just the two of us, Ma, go ahead ...

PATRICIA:
Maybe once I've finished my story.

RICHARD:
The journalists here were so obviously delighted to report it, it was disgusting ... Not one of them was there, of course, but they speculated and they decreed, they predicted and they passed judgement wildly ... I called a couple of them, the ones who were most vicious, most unfair, what did you say your name was, they asked, more or less dismissing me ... They weren't interested in hearing someone defend her, they wanted people to lay it on, to drag her name in the mud, to predict her downfall or, at least, her decline! That's more interesting than good news. When something good happens to a Québécois artist abroad, there's always a negative reason, but when it's something bad, it's always justified.

PATRICIA:
I could just imagine what the papers here would say ...

MICHELLE:
You're right, it was pretty bad ...

PATRICIA:
Never imagining what was in store for me.

MICHELLE:
So what haven't you told me, Ma?

PATRICIA:
My agent was in the process of negotiating next season ... I don't have to tell you that my dance card isn't as full as it used to be, I'm no longer booked two or three years in advance, the way I was for almost twenty years. I still have my faithful audience, but there are younger singers breathing down my

28

neck, and slander's a great weapon. I think the opera world is even more of a cliché than others ... And the cruelty is worse because it's cruelty devoid of any intelligence ... Anyway, two days later ... I was singing Musetta in *La Bohème* ... It was my turn to replace a fat Russian singer ... I said yes immediately, because I knew I had to get back on stage as fast as possible to prove I wouldn't break up every time I performed ... Musetta is easy, it's gratifying, everybody loves you, especially when you sing that stupid little waltz all opera singers learn to hate six months into their career, but the audiences never seem to grow tired of it, who knows why ... Anyway ... I sang Musetta, I was brilliant, better than the Mimi, actually, a bland Bulgarian with no personality who probably couldn't be heard beyond the tenth row but she has the face of an angel. I didn't hit any false notes, I was showered with compliments, everybody was happy ... Then ... let me catch my breath, I'm so furious ...

MICHELLE:
You want something to drink? I made sure there was some orange juice, a bottle of mineral water—

PATRICIA:
No, thanks, we'll open it when you grandmother gets here, it might shut her up for a few minutes ...
Alright ... I may as well get it off my chest right away.

RICHARD:
Unfortunately, the journalists were right ... and that's why I got the famous phone call.

PATRICIA:
When I got back to my dressing room after *La Bohème*, there was an official letter from the Opéra Bastille waiting for me. I thought, great, next year's schedule, I'll finally know if they're remounting *Salomé* or not ... Well, they're remounting *Salomé* alright ... but they had the nerve to offer me the role

of Herodias, the scheming mother! Do you realise what it means, in my world, when they start asking a singer to sing Herodias?

MICHELLE:

Not really …

PATRICIA:

Herodias is a role for singers on their way out … Oh, it's a good role, it's gratifying, it's the Musetta for aging singers … When you start having serious voice problems, over sixty, or earlier if you're unlucky … you're happy to sing Herodias, it's noble when you're the one who chooses, everyone understands, they think: "Another legend who wants to bow out discreetly, it's fantastic, even if she bleats like a goat, let's applaud her courage and salute her longevity." Léonie Rysanek sang it until she was over seventy! She was still singing it on her death bed, for chrissakes! But when they *offer* you Herodias … It's every singer's nightmare—will the day come when they offer me Herodias before I choose it myself? And they dared offer it to me at my age! I'm not even fifty! I cried so hard over that letter on Opéra Bastille letterhead, you have no idea … Me, singing Herodias as of next year! And all because of one false note brought on by a case of the giggles! I could see Myriam Ange-Bell push me aside and step onto the stage in my place! In my place. I could see the headlines: "The Paris Opera presents two Canadian divas for the price of one!" "Battle of the Maria Chapdelaines!" "Two Lady Lumberjacks storm the Bastille!"

MICHELLE:

Ma, c'mon!

PATRICIA:

I'd stripped on stage two nights earlier because I'm still presentable and desirable—name me one other

30

singer who still dares take off her clothes on stage at my age—and they were sidelining me because of one little mistake!

RICHARD:

It's true the critics had noted some serious problems with her voice recently. And the more reliable ones, who hardly mentioned her breaking up and the false note, said that she had had problems all evening, that her medium range was all over the place, even though her high and low notes were still beautiful ... Patricia Pasquetti has been in decline for the past couple of years, despite her relatively young age, there's no denying it, but that's no reason to get rid of her like that, with no warning, no notice.

PATRICIA:

I had to make a move, fast!

RICHARD:

It's worse than cruel, it's vicious.

PATRICIA:

And I made a move, fast! They didn't have to wait for my answer. I turned on a dime, as your grandmother would say. Speaking of whom, where is she, anyway?

MICHELLE:

She had a rehearsal, too.

PATRICIA:

So I'm less important than a rehearsal for her, too. In the opera, we show up a few days before the performance, we meet our partners, we work a bit with the conductor, the director—have I ever told you how much I hate directors who *revisit* operas I've been performing for thirty years? Carmen is a gypsy, for godssake, she's not some hooker from the Spanish Civil War wearing a Basque beret and a soldier's overcoat. Anyway, we try on our costumes, we complain because we're never satisfied, and most of the time with good reason, then the show goes on. We walk onto the stage, we hardly know where to stand—but who cares the follow spot will find us—and no one notices a thing! It's only when *Aïda* takes place during the Gulf War that the audience notices! And they don't like it either! But let's not get started on that again, I know you don't agree with me, and it turned sour the last time we had that discussion.

MICHELLE:

The reason you never want to rehearse is that you're always singing the same damn things!

PATRICIA:

I said let's change the subject.

MICHELLE:

But I'm telling you, there are times when rehearsing would help! Like that time you came to sing Manon at the Montreal Opera and you almost fell down a hole in the final desert set—

PATRICIA:

Michelle! I said that's enough.

MICHELLE:

You're a bunch of lazy spoiled brats, that's what you are!

PATRICIA:

Michelle!

MICHELLE:

(sarcastically) Sure, go on with your story, it's much more interesting!

PATRICIA:

Where was I? You've confused me now.

MICHELLE:

You turned on a dime …

PATRICIA:

Exactly, girl, you know me! I turned on nothing and I called Richard ...

RICHARD:

When she called me, *when she called me to her rescue,* she was so hysterical I could hardly understand what she was saying.

PATRICIA:

He was so surprised to hear from me, you know, he was there at the other end of line, hardly saying a word ... I think he might've been crying!

RICHARD:

And like an idiot, I was crying like a baby because I thought she'd finally gone round the bend! I've heard her rant and rave before, but never like that!

PATRICIA:

I'd had a good idea, but I wasn't sure he understood me, and it was important for him to understand because I absolutely needed him!

RICHARD:

She'd had this crazy idea and I was supposed to say yes to everything she was asking ... And I ended up saying yes to everything ... I've never known how to refuse her anything, I've never known how to hold my own with her, to defend my point of view, to say no ...

PATRICIA:

I thought he'd say yes right away as usual, that he'd hang up and I'd go meet him at Charles de Gaulle airport the next morning, but instead ... I had to explain it to him a hundred times, I had to beg him, promise him I don't know what, probably more money, before he finally accepted to get on a plane the following night.

RICHARD:

She'd decided to give an impromptu recital somewhere, anywhere, in some rented hall she hadn't even found yet, to prove to Paris and the rest of the world that she could still sing Salomé, and Aïda, and Butterfly, and Mimi ... And most of all, to prove that Herodias was still a long way away! It was a beautiful idea, actually, but it was crazy!

PATRICIA:

It was a good idea, wasn't it? I wanted to take them by surprise, catch them short them in the middle of their sarcastic comments, to astonish them and make them swallow their insinuations, by singing all the most difficult roles with just a piano to accompany me.

RICHARD:

And the piano, obviously, had to be me! I told you earlier, all she has to do is call, and I come running like a little puppy dog! And I came running like a little puppy dog, as usual, my sheet music under one arm, my duffel bag slung over the other!

PATRICIA:

I had given myself 48 hours to find a hall ...

RICHARD:

I didn't even know where she was going to hold the recital ...

PATRICIA:

You know that's not easy in a city like Paris ...

RICHARD:

She'd told me she was prepared to sing on the steps of the Bastille Opera House with a parrot on her shoulder and a begging bowl in her hand, and I knew she was capable of doing just that!

PATRICIA:
I was prepared to sing at the Brasserie Boffinger if necessary, they owe it to me, I spend my half my fees in that place. They have customers who show up just to watch me assassinate a dozen oysters ...

RICHARD:
I knew we wouldn't even have time to rehearse ...

PATRICIA:
I knew that with Richard, one quick little rehearsal would do the trick ... He drives me crazy, he's hysterical, he's never satisfied, but we've been working together for so long we can communicate with a glance once we're on stage ... And he's a helluva good accompanist, you know that, you've seen him often enough ...

RICHARD:
I wasn't about to perform in Paris unrehearsed!

PATRICIA:
But there wasn't a single damn hall free in all of Paris! Kiri was singing at the Champs-Élysées, and I'm telling you, that one has more problems with her voice than me! Placido was parading his over-sixty self at the Bastille in one of Verdi's early operas, a pompous thing nobody except him still dares to sing—if he's allowed to hit all the false notes he wants, why can't I—my Bulgarian Mimi was bleating at Gaveau Hall, so it'd reached the point I was about to call Boffinger's—I swear, I was serious, I would have done it—and Kiri, Placido and Mimi never would have been able to beat that publicity stunt—when I thought of calling the Centre culturel at the Canadian Embassy ... They don't have a concert hall, but they've got a helluva beautiful garden!

RICHARD:

She stormed into the Centre culturel on Wednesday and she was singing on Thursday. I don't think they knew what hit them!

PATRICIA:

I arrived on their doorstep Wednesday morning and announced that I was giving a free recital there the following evening. I was on the phone before they had time to say no.

RICHARD:

The news spread like wildfire, you can imagine ... Patricia Pasquetti singing for free ... not something that happens every day ... But there were other concerts scheduled that same night ...

PATRICIA:

A half hour later everything was rented.

RICHARD:

Two hours later, everything was rented! But we should have known better ... I don't know ... checked out who'd be coming ... I arrived Thursday morning, the day of the recital ... I hadn't slept all night, I was in full jetlag, and I had to accompany Madame that same evening!

PATRICIA:

Richard thrives on pressure. He's the nervous type, so that's how you have to treat him.

RICHARD:

I thought she'd send a taxi, but she came to get me in person. The minute I walked through customs, I saw this ball of fur smelling of *L'air du temps* rushing towards me, waving her arms. She was so wound up she even carried my suitcase. She tore it away from me like it was something obscene, and she rushed ahead saying the movers were already setting up the piano in the garden at the Centre culturel. I felt like stretching out on the floor at the airport to take a little nap, but that was out of the question!

PATRICIA:

I went to the trouble of picking him up at the airport in person, I brought him back to my place to freshen up, and he still managed to find something to complain about.

RICHARD:

I had less than a half hour to freshen up and get ready, and we took off for the rehearsal! We had less than twelve hours to go before the recital. I've never been through anything like it!

PATRICIA:

He started complaining about his stomach, as usual, and he swallowed a couple of Diovol. Then he felt nauseous because he hadn't chewed them enough ...

RICHARD:

She was so uptight, she was shouting so loud, and talking so fast I thought she was going to blow a fuse and then she wouldn't be able to sing that night. I was too slow for her ...

PATRICIA:

You know what a pain he can be when he's in one of his slow moods...

RICHARD:

She thought I looked too pale ...

PATRICIA:

And he was white as a sheet. I was afraid he'd collapse onto the keyboard after playing three bars ...

RICHARD:

She said my tux smelled of the dry cleaner's ...

PATRICIA:

His tux reeked of the dry cleaner's ...

RICHARD:
... even through the plastic cover!

PATRICIA:
... through the plastic cover! I could smell it through the plastic, do you believe it?! Are the dry cleaners here still so hard on your clothes?

RICHARD:
She was ordering me around like I was a servant hired for the day ...

PATRICIA:
He just stood there with his arms at his side and his mouth hanging open, like he didn't understand a thing I way saying, so I had to yell at him!

RICHARD:
She was despicable the whole day!

PATRICIA:
Really, I had to drag him around behind me like a ball and chain the whole damn day! I almost regretted having flown him across the Atlantic! I thought maybe I should have accompanied myself on the piano, like when I can't find an accompanist for my rehearsals ...

RICHARD:
She threatened to give the recital on her own, she told me I was useless, that I was *always* useless, an amateur, unreliable and totally ungrateful for everything she's done for me, that she'd wasted an airplane ticket on me for nothing ...

PATRICIA:
God, I'd dragged him out of his hole and given him a chance to accompany me *in Paris* for one of the most important recitals of my life, *I was calling him to my rescue,* that doesn't happen every day, and all he could do was complain!

MICHELLE laughs.

PATRICIA:
Why are you laughing?

MICHELLE:
I'd love to hear his version of the story!

PATRICIA:
His version? Everyone would feel sorry for him and I'd be the bad guy, as usual! He always manages to make people feel sorry for him. Listen, I'm used to it. How many years have we been working together, whenever I'm back here … twelve years?

RICHARD:
And you should have heard the piano! I admit we got there before the tuner, but still! I felt like I was playing an old honky tonk piano! I'm not kidding. They must've dragged it out of some damp cellar! I kept thinking, of course, she'll sound like she's singing in tune compared to that!

PATRICIA:
I admit the piano was a bit out of tune at first, but the tuner came and fixed that, and then we realized that even if it wasn't exceptional, it was a perfectly fine instrument.

RICHARD:
So who was the amateur, I ask you? I kept thinking, she wants to commit suicide and she's determined to drag me down with her, this is ridiculous, *no self-respecting professional singer, not even the most desperate, would give a recital in these conditions!* She was so devoured by her anger and her need for revenge, I think she'd forgotten she was supposed to sing that evening! I started calling her, the Electra of Nuns' Island, in my head, and I almost said it to her face. But she probably would've replied that I made a pathetic Orestes and she would've been right … I should've said it anyway, right? Whatever. The people

from the Centre culturel just stared at her, speechless, I don't think they'd ever seen the likes of her.

Silence.

Change of pace.

PATRICIA:
But no matter how much I yell at him, no matter how much I complain about him … when he sits down at the piano, that damn guy …

RICHARD:
But everything straightened itself out when I sat down at the piano, when we started rehearsing, even though it was still out of tune … there's something …

PATRICIA:
There's something between us …

RICHARD:
Between us …

PATRICIA:
It's hard to explain …

RICHARD:
Something that can't be explained … I could try, right now, to describe what happened when I sat down at the piano … but I wouldn't succeed.

PATRICIA:
I've never seen anything like it …

RICHARD:
You can't put it into words …

PATRICIA:
I've never seen a more talented accompanist. Not even in the biggest cities in Europe …

RICHARD:
Maybe it's just …

PATRICIA:

And believe me there's no shortage of pianists ...

RICHARD:

I don't know ...

PATRICIA:

But when we make music together, the two of us ...

RICHARD:

Maybe it's just that when we make music together ...

PATRICIA:

... something happens ...

RICHARD:

... something inexpressible happens between us ...

PATRICIA:

... something unique that I can't put into words ...

MICHELLE:

I know I've heard the two of you dozens of times ...

PATRICIA:

It's true, isn't it? Admit that it's ... absolutely unique.

MICHELLE:

Yes, it is.

RICHARD:

Now I don't want you to think it's easy! It isn't. Far from it. It's hard work, it's difficult, demanding ... But when I sit down at the piano and Madame Pasquetti takes her place for the rehearsal or the recital ...

PATRICIA comes to stand beside the piano.

We hear the first bars of Schubert's Serenade, Ständchen D 957.4.

RICHARD and PATRICIA listen to each other sing and play.

41

RICHARD:

If you only knew ... If you knew ... Everything
disappears, completely, like in a fog ...

PATRICIA:

Everything disappears ...

RICHARD:

Nothing else exists except the voice and the piano ...

PATRICIA:

Nothing.

RICHARD:

I wouldn't call what I feel in those moments pleasure
... it's beyond pleasure ... It requires constant
concentration, I have to watch what I'm playing, and
how Madame Pasquetti is singing, because what I do
and what she does isn't always exactly the same, we're
human beings, not machines. I have to follow her
without letting it show, without ever getting ahead of
her or behind her ... It's ... a fantastic state! Some
people think we must see beautiful images, that we
make up beautiful movies or that we tell ourselves
beautiful stories, that we paint beautiful pictures in
our heads when we play piano ... but it's not true!
We have to work at it. And it's hard! All we can see is
where we are in the piece, and our level of concentration and control ... and if a drop of sweat runs
down your nose or a tear wells up in your eyes—
because sometimes we get tears in our eyes, not tears
of emotion, but tears of satisfaction and relief, tears
of joy, joy that has nothing to do with pleasure—if
that happens, you can't wipe the sweat or brush away
the tear, you have to ignore it and carry on, because
you can't leave the keyboard for a single second, you
have to pretend that the sweat or the tear doesn't
exist. It's the same for Madame Pasquetti ... When
she looks like she's in ecstasy, it doesn't necessarily
mean she thinks she's great, it might be to hide a

mistake, blur a note that's a bit off. I'm sure if we asked her she'd say, too, that it's not a question of pleasure, it's more than pleasure, it has nothing to do with pleasure.

PATRICIA:

The pleasure of singing with him ... I feel ... carried away by the music ... as if there were a wind at my back ... there's complete osmosis between us. I feel as if I'm floating on the music! I never lose control, and he never loses control! We move forward together, in perfect harmony! What a pleasure!

RICHARD:

But maybe I'm too intense ... Sometimes I watch another pianist play in a concert or on television in a close-up, and I say to myself: how come he looks truly ecstatic! Is he really? Does he really feel as if he's going to swoon with pleasure, is he really as ecstatic as he looks? Where is he, right now? How come I never feel like that? I'd love to look like that when I play! Actually, not look like that because sometimes it's so exaggerated they look like idiots, but I'd like to *feel* what they feel, if they really feel it! But I don't believe it! I don't believe it because no matter how much they love what they're doing, they're working, and working hard! But maybe it's just me. Maybe it's me who can't let go!

PATRICIA:

It was an extraordinary concert. The weather was perfect, it was packed, the garden at the Centre culturel was exquisite, the audience was in bliss ... I did them all ... all the big hits of my career. One after another ... Aïda, Butterfly, Manon Lescaut, La Marschalin, Santuzza, Norma ... Norma in the light of a real moon, Michelle, it's incredible! And Salomé. I didn't need John the Baptist's head to make them shudder. With horror and pleasure at the same time.

Richard handled it like a real pro, we've worked on those scores so often, for so many years, so obsessively, I'd say, that I'm sure it showed. Not a single error all evening! His piano resonated inside those stone walls, my voice rose into the Parisian night, I could see people open their eyes in amazement when I delivered a particularly beautiful or emphatic note ... A pure joy!

RICHARD:

But to get back to Madame Pasquetti ... How can I put it? It was an evening ... I can't find the right word ... of delusion! That's it! She spun a web of self-delusion, and she was determined to believe in it!

PATRICIA:

A pure joy!

RICHARD:

The whole thing was terribly sad, actually ...

PATRICIA:

In less than two hours, I had erased everything!

RICHARD:

Terribly sad ...

PATRICIA:

I cleared my name, my voice, my art ...

RICHARD:

I think she experienced the evening she wanted to experience, but not the one that took place ...

PATRICIA:

I left there ready to confront every Myriam Ange-Bell in the world! The reception was a total bore, but it didn't matter. I'd done what I had to do, and I didn't mind flitting through the crowd of nobodies, acting cute, like a queen slumming it ...

RICHARD:

> Fortunately, a couple of her fans had heard about the recital and had shown up at the very last minute. They kept her busy for a while with their shrill voices and their ridiculous adjectives ... They were *mesmerized,* and *devastated with happiness,* and *moved to the core of their beings!* Honestly!

PATRICIA:

> My fans were there, but you know how exhausting that can be, those hard-core fans who follow you everywhere and always expect you to fuss over them ...

MICHELLE:

> No, Ma, I wouldn't know ...

PATRICIA:

> Oh, of course! Sorry! I should've realized! Boy, how dumb can I get, sometimes ... Anyway, I took their compliments with a grain of salt ... maybe I was just barely polite. But they love that ... If you're too nice ... I don't know ... if you're too nice, you're human, and a diva is supposed to be anything but human!

RICHARD:

> Obviously, the minute the recital was over, she started being obnoxious with me again ... Why? Why does she do it? She always treats me like her servant! Richard, fetch this, Richard, fetch that, she shoves me around, she pushes me aside when we run into someone important, she interrupts me in the middle of my conversations ... she even went so far as to tell me, in the middle of the reception in front of everyone, that I hadn't always played in tune ... precisely at the points when she was the one who made a mistake!

PATRICIA:

But Richard got on my nerves something awful ...
Every time he spotted a guy who looked remotely
interesting, he'd pounce on him like a cat on a
mouse ...

RICHARD:

I'm fed up!

PATRICIA:

You know how he can be ...

RICHARD:

I can't take it anymore!

PATRICIA:

A real weather vane! He falls in love every fifteen
minutes and, *even worse*, he's heartbroken every half
hour! God, it's exhausting, people who can't restrain
themselves!

RICHARD:

I refuse to be treated like that anymore!

PATRICIA:

And it's so obvious when he's interested in someone,
he's so un-subtle, I'm ashamed of him.

RICHARD:

I'm ashamed of putting up with it ...

PATRICIA:

It's very simple, he got on my nerves so bad last
night, I ignored him during the entire flight today.

MICHELLE:

I don't understand why you decided to come home,
Ma ...

PATRICIA:

What?

MICHELLE:

Why did you decide to come home? Why didn't you
stay and enjoy your triumph?

46

PATRICIA:
I don't know. A whim. This isn't my first whim, is it?

MICHELLE:
Nor the last ...

PATRICIA:
I'd seen enough of them ... I thought ... Maybe if I disappear from Paris for a week ... I don't have any engagements for the next ten days, and then it's on the other side of the planet ... maybe if I disappear, having triumphed, leaving them ecstatic ... let them stew in their juices for a while, let them come looking for me, it will do them good! When the director of the Bastille reads the reviews, he'll eat his copy of the letter he dared write me!

RICHARD suddenly stands up.

RICHARD:
Why am I telling you all this?!

PATRICIA:
As usual, Richard sat there looking like a whipped dog ...

RICHARD:
You're not the one I should be telling this to!

PATRICIA:
His hound dog look ...

RICHARD:
She is!

PATRICIA:
I'm not kidding, I could've punched him ...

RICHARD:
I should be saying this to her!

PATRICIA:
That guy's got no nerve ...

RICHARD:
My three quarters of an hour must be up now, right?

PATRICIA:
No guts …

RICHARD:
It must've been three quarters of an hour by now.

PATRICIA:
No balls …

RICHARD:
(taking the money out of his pocket) Here, here's the
money for today's session … I'm going to go tell her,
to her face!

He puts the money down on the piano.

PATRICIA:
He might be a great musician, but, what can I say,
he's got no balls!

MICHELLE:
Oh, get off his back, Ma!

RICHARD:
I think I'll have the courage to do it today! I've never
been so worked up, so ready to talk to her. I've always
lost my nerve when I'm with her, but now …

PATRICIA:
Easy for you to say! You're not the one who has to
put up with him!

MICHELLE:
He has to put up with you, too! And believe me,
that's not easy!

RICHARD:
I'm sure you're going to tell me one session like this
isn't enough, that I'll lose my nerve at the last
minute, that I'll swallow my pride in front of her, as
usual … But you're wrong. I can feel it. I can feel the
nerve! Thank you! Thanks for listening to me, it did

me a lot of good, but I don't think I'll be needing
you anymore.

He rushes off, exalted, feverish.

PATRICIA:
I don't know if Maria had a pain in the ass like him
... Probably did ...

MICHELLE:
Leave Maria out of this.

PATRICIA:
What?

MICHELLE:
Leave Maria Callas out of this!

PATRICIA:
What makes you say that all of a sudden?

MICHELLE:
You talk about her as if you grew up on the same
street together! You never even met Maria Callas!

PATRICIA:
I beg your pardon. That's not true! They introduced
her to me the last time she was at the Place des Arts,
right here in Montreal!

MICHELLE:
C'mon! She wasn't introduced to you, *you* were
introduced to her! It's not the same thing. When
your famous foreign conductor passed through town
and discovered you in the early eighties at a Montreal
Symphony concert, Maria Callas had already been
dead for five years! The last time she came to
Montreal in the seventies, you were still one of the
nobodies you despise so much today! And you made
fun of her for years, imitating the two of them, her
and Giuseppe di Stefano, when he accompanied her
on her last world tour.

PATRICIA:

Maria was younger than I am when she died, and
she'd lost her voice long before that. And, excuse
me, but I can call Maria Callas anything I want! I
don't get it ... Call me stupid if you want, but I don't
get why you're bringing all this up now ...

MICHELLE:

Because I'm fed up with your goddamn
namedropping, that's why!

PATRICIA:

Namedropping! What namedropping? What are you
talking about?

MICHELLE:

Ma, give me a break, don't play innocent! Whenever
you come home from a trip, even if you don't like us
to use the word trip, since you claim you're a citizen
of the world—

PATRICIA:

And it's true!

MICHELLE:

Whenever you come home from a trip, you bend our
ears about Kiri and Placido, about Renée, Luciano
and José, or Birgitt, Claudio, Riccardo—

PATRICIA:

What do you expect me to call them? Those are their
names!

MICHELLE:

And you really lay it on when you're with your old
friends, rubbing their noses in your great fame, you
dazzle them with all sorts of supposedly innocent
anecdotes, that you only tell to remind them, the
Montreal nobodies, that *you* hang out with the great
of this world, that you're on a first name basis with
the greatest stars, that you've had lunch at Renée
Fleming's house, that you had to put up with Luciano

Pavarotti's garlic breath, that you were courted by
Simon Keenlyside who's twenty years younger than
you, while the most famous conductor they know is
young Nezet-Séguin! Well, we're so out of it here, Ma,
we don't even know who Simon Keenlyside is!

PATRICIA:
Ah ha! So, you're the one who feels frustrated, right
... Poor kid ...

MICHELLE:
Alright, maybe it does bother me. It's true, my
friends don't have first names known around the
world, but we still have time ... But your friends, Ma,
it makes them feel bad. It humiliates them. If that's
the point of the exercise, then you really succeed!
Congratulations!

PATRICIA:
My friends are happy for me—

MICHELLE:
Your friends make fun of you behind your back! They
get so fed up whenever you're around, they can
hardly wait to see you leave, they can hardly wait to
see you leave so they can badmouth you!

PATRICIA:
You don't know what you're saying—

MICHELLE:
Fine ... If you prefer to believe that—

PATRICIA:
What do you expect me to do? When I come back
after eight months, like today? What am I supposed
to say, once I've asked them how they are? Once I've
asked them how things are going here? I know how
things are going here, Michelle, nothing ever
changes. It's always the same! Frozen in time! I know
what they're going to say: Oh, there's nothing new ...

So I don't ask anymore! They chose to stay here, that's not my fault, dammit!

MICHELLE:

There's no shame in staying here! What do you expect us to do? Beg your forgiveness for being so insignificant! I haven't yet met my famous foreign director, Ma! What do you expect me to do about it? I graduated from the National Theatre School not so long ago, I've had a couple of interesting roles, but I'm almost thirty and there still hasn't been a famous foreign director who's ecstatic about my acting and has asked me to join his company and travel around the world! Sorry, but that's how it is, that's the sad truth. You were over thirty, and as bitchy as they come when the miracle happened to you, Ma. So give me time, who knows, maybe lady luck will come knocking on this family's door again! I might hit the jackpot when I least expect it!

PATRICIA:

You have no excuse, you had every opportunity to succeed—

MICHELLE:

What do you mean … I had every opportunity to succeed? Just because you dragged me around Europe like your pet monkey during part of my childhood doesn't mean I had every opportunity to succeed! I was so miserable living in those hotel rooms, I was a real brat!

PATRICIA:

You had the choice of the best schools in the world! You could've studied in Switzerland like the Grimaldi princesses, and the daughters of the great, if you'd wanted to!

MICHELLE:

I wasn't interested in that, Ma!

PATRICIA:
No! You preferred to come back here with your
father! How is your father, anyway? Still in the
baritone section of the Montreal Opera Chorus?

MICHELLE:
I don't have to answer a blow below the belt like that.

PATRICIA:
You're right, I'm sorry ... When I mention him, I lose
my cool.

MICHELLE:
And I suppose that in your opinion, he had every
opportunity to succeed, too?

PATRICIA:
He certainly did! I came back to get him, I came
back to get both of you I don't know how many times
... I had connections for him, he was a good singer,
he could have followed me—

MICHELLE:
Did it ever occur to you that we liked it here?

PATRICIA:
Impossible! It's impossible to like it here.

MICHELLE:
And I'm sure it never occurred to you that we didn't
feel like being either the daughter or the husband of
the great Patricia Pasquetti, that it was humiliating,
especially for him who never had a famous foreign
director in his life either, and who refused to have his
wife as his mentor!

PATRICIA:
It's impossible to like it here, *it's too small!* Do you
realize how small it is here, Michelle? Do you? Look
out the window, look across the river ... It looks like a
big city, there's lots of big buildings, lots of noise and
pollution! But if you only realized how small it is
once you manage to get away!

MICHELLE:

How can you say that?

PATRICIA:

I can say it because I think it! The farther away you get, the more you realize how insignificant this place is! When you arrive in a real big city, a civilised city that matters culturally, and they ask you where you come from and you answer, from Montreal, they frown and scratch their heads, they can vaguely remember Expo, the Place des Arts, the snow and the cold, the Olympic stadium that looks like a toilet bowl, and Céline Dion's accent. They were happy just to pass through Montreal, and they can't say it left a lasting impression! Well, that's when you're happy you got away! It's so small here, Michelle, nothing important ever happens here! Nothing that makes a difference! Culturally or otherwise! Everything important happens somewhere else, comes from somewhere else! Whether you like it or not, that's how it is! *Wake up, my dear girl!* Just because your father decided to bury himself alive here doesn't mean you have to follow in his footsteps!

MICHELLE:

I don't feel like I'm buried alive here, Ma! You should take a better look at this town yourself. Your husband's carved out an enviable position for himself here, Ma, he's a respected baritone, and your daughter's trying to do the same thing, trying to become a respected actor! Even if our daily routine doesn't include breakfast with Hildegard Behrens or tea with Patrick Dupont.

PATRICIA:

That's a pity, because if there ever was a fabulous host, it's Patrick Dupont—

MICHELLE:

That's not the point! Maybe it is true that the best thing I can hope for is a lead role at Théâtre du Nouveau Monde once in a while, or a Radio Canada TV series that will last as long as possible so I can make a half-decent living! Or maybe I can create a new play with a bunch of friends, a new work, Ma, something I watched grow from nothing, from an idea by a writer my own age, someone I studied with at the Theatre School, something that took shape slowly, made us sick with worry and doubt, and finally landed us on a little stage in a small theatre, with our friends and family who'd come to encourage us and suddenly they're thrilled because they've just witnessed the birth of a new play! A new play, Ma! A play that might not get produced three hundred years from now, but something I helped create! Does that make me an artist of less significance, an artist who's less important, less interesting just because I haven't performed in a great classic at the Comédie française?! What's more important—to flop like you did in *Nabucco* at La Scala or to do a decent job here?

PATRICIA:

I beg your pardon, I didn't flop in *Nabucco* at La Scala—

MICHELLE:

Yes, you did flop in *Nabucco* at La Scala. For once, let's call a spade a spade. Abigail never was a role for your voice, and you ruined your voice because you were determined to sing it anyway! They booed you, they practically threw you off the stage and you know it, Ma!

PATRICIA:

Is that what the papers said here?

MICHELLE:
That's what the papers said everywhere, Ma! In
Europe, in the States, and probably in Timbuktu ...
But that's not the point, either.

PATRICIA:
Yes, it is. That is precisely the point! You have to
admit it's more interesting to ruin your voice at La
Scala than at *l'Opéra de Montréal!*

MICHELLE:
No, it isn't! The important thing is not to ruin your
voice! Period!

PATRICIA:
It's impossible to have a discussion with you. You mix
everything up and I forget what I'm saying. Obviously
the important thing is not to ruin your voice,
everyone knows that and everyone agrees on that! As
usual, you make me sound stupid ... What I mean ...
What I mean is that, if I'm going to risk my voice, I'd
rather risk it big-time, in a place that matters instead
of some backwater where nobody notices if you're
out of tune or not!

MICHELLE:
Don't say it doesn't matter here, Ma, it matters to me.
This backwater is important to me. And it's big
enough for me, too!

PATRICIA:
Well, that's too bad, dear, too bad for you! Okay, let's
change the subject! What can I say? You're
determined to stay here, what I can do about that?
Nothing! So stay! Arggh, you know how to get a
woman's vacation off to a great start! With a
provincial attitude like that, you won't go very far in
life, believe me.

MICHELLE:
You're the one with the provincial attitude, Ma—

PATRICIA:

> Now that's a lie!

MICHELLE:

> You're the one who's been carrying on like a hick for the past twenty years, trying to impress the people who matter, as you say, the people who make a difference! At least, here I don't have to deny anything. You've denied your roots for them. You changed your name for them! When you left town, your name was Patricia Paquette, and when you stepped off the plane the next morning in Florence, because there's where it all began, at the May Festival in Florence, your name was Patricia Pasquetti! Poof! Seven hours on a plane, and a new woman was born! You changed your accent for them, and you only revive it when you come home or when you want to amuse Claudio Abbado or Riccardo Muti! You'd rather massage the corners of your mouth in your hotel room every night!

PATRICIA:

> It's not true that I've denied my roots. I've always said I come from Lac Saint-Jean! Wherever I go! Just like Kiri has always said she's Maori! But can you imagine, a rehearsal on the stage at the Paris Opera with a diva who has a Québécois accent? *(exaggerating her accent)* Excuse me, maestro, I don't *tink* I understood what you said to me.

MICHELLE:

> Why not?

PATRICIA:

> That's ridiculous! The minute I arrive in Europe, it's automatic, something changes in my mouth, my vowels get longer, my diction gets clearer, and I talk like them. It's normal.

57

MICHELLE:
> You love being the first one to do something! So why not be the first one to change that!

PATRICIA:
> You don't know what you're talking about ... We're not just talking about leaving a small town for a bigger one, we're talking about the most sophisticated, the most snobbish, the most cultivated scene in the world. No one would dare trot out the accent from his native village on stage in Bayreuth, impossible! Wagner would roll over in his grave!

MICHELLE:
> It might do him a lot of good! Maybe shake off some of the dust!

PATRICIA:
> Let's not get started on that, okay, we've gone over that enough times in the past ten years ... Our discussions are always dead ends, Michelle, because neither one of us ever wants to give an inch.

MICHELLE:
> We live on different planets, Ma.

PATRICIA:
> You said it, not me. *(moving a bit closer, quietly)* How is your father? Really?

MICHELLE:
> He's really fine, Ma. Boring, isn't it? Starting a new family, at his age, and he's perfectly happy—

PATRICIA:
> Mid-life crisis.

MICHELLE:
> Call it what you want, it suits him! He's got a six-month-old son and he's crazy about him! Do you believe it?! I've got a six-month-old half-brother. I still can't get over it.

PATRICIA shrugs.

PATRICIA:

(*sarcastically*) Does he still support the Parti
Québécois? Is there another referendum coming up
soon? Are you all about to miss another rendezvous
with history?

MICHELLE:

You didn't always sing that tune.

PATRICIA:

In a previous lifetime, no.

MICHELLE:

It wasn't that long ago, Ma. In my bedroom I still
have a picture of René Lévesque holding me in his
arms, the night the Parti Québécois came into power
... and I'm crying like an idiot because I was afraid of
him.

PATRICIA:

That's what I mean, in a previous lifetime—

MICHELLE:

And you're standing beside us, gazing at your god in
adoration ... Was he your Claudio Abbado at the
time?

PATRICIA:

Let's drop the subject, Michelle, that's all over.

MICHELLE:

If everyone acts like you, it's all over for sure.

PATRICIA:

When I remember all that ...

She sighs.

MICHELLE:

You're not going to tell me you're ashamed when you
remember all that?

PATRICIA stares at MICHELLE for a moment before
answering.

PATRICIA:

It was all a dream. I was young, I had an afro, and I'd never left home. I'm not ashamed, Michelle, on the contrary, I'm pretty proud of everything I did in those days, but it's ... I don't know ... it feels like it happened to someone else, not me.

MICHELLE:

So aren't you proud to see all that in your daughter?

PATRICIA:

(after a silence) No.

MICHELLE:

Why not?

PATRICIA:

Because it will produce still another disillusioned person.

MICHELLE:

Maybe not!

PATRICIA:

Oh, yes, Michelle, yes, it will.

MICHELLE:

But that's how I was raised, Ma! You trained me like that! I was weaned on the slogans, I grew up in the middle of a perpetual party with all the nationalists who gathered at our house, all those people you and Dad fed practically every night of the week. It was like a year-round open house. They'd bring the wine, you'd supply the grub. THE GRUB! I swear that's when the expression was born! When Pauline Julien came to the house, you'd tell her how beautifully out of tune she sang, and that you envied her because what she was singing was so *alive,* and she'd laugh. She was your idol. You told her that's what everyone should sing, that those were the songs that would save us, not Wagner or Verdi or Gilbert and Sullivan! Monique Leyrac, Renée Claude and Isabelle Pierre would play full-blast on our stereo all day long, and the rest of them, too, the singers your father used to call the guitar pluckers because he couldn't stand them. I was two years old in 1976, and I was six during the first referendum, and you used to drag me along everywhere, saying you had to prepare the next generation! I hope you haven't forgotten that.

PATRICIA:

No, I haven't forgotten. I haven't forgotten any of it. I never said I'd forgotten.

MICHELLE:

You took me to Québec City with you, in the charter bus with all the Artists for YES in 1980. I stood behind you on the stage at the Palais des Congrès in Québec City when you went up to the mic and said: "Patricia Paquette, opera singer!" And during the ovation, you held the mic in front of me and I said shyly: "Michelle Paquette-Beaulieu, opera singer's daughter! Yes!", while they were still applauding! I was six years old. Do you think I realized what I was saying? I didn't have any choice, Ma, I never had a choice. I never reached a point in my life when I said to myself: this is what we should believe in, this is how things should be, *you drilled it into me without my asking!* I have trouble thinking for myself, because it's a sin! It's a sin to think any other way! At least, that's what I've always thought … But here we are, twenty years later, and the woman responsible for it all, the instigator of all that, the one who raised me, shaped me, showed me how to think what she thought, tells me that it was just a dream and there's no use pursuing it!

61

PATRICIA:

I didn't say there was no use pursuing it. I guess ... I guess it's alright to go on if you're stuck here ... but you don't understand—

MICHELLE:

What?! I don't understand what!

PATRICIA:

I told you a while ago, it's one of the first things I said.. Listen ... Almost immediately after the referendum ... First Duplessis and the Great Darkness, then the Great Flop! Anyway ... That's when, you know that, that's when I was ... let's say, discovered, immediately after the referendum. I was singing with the symphony orchestra, I was performing a cycle of songs by Berlioz, *Les nuits d'été*, even if I wasn't old enough, and probably didn't yet have the voice, but the conductor saw something in me ... but that's not what I wanted to say—

MICHELLE:

I hope not!

PATRICIA:

I just wanted to say ... but you know that, too ... I just wanted to say ... When you're up to your neck in a problem, it's hard to see beyond the tip of your nose, but as soon as you get some perspective ... You have to understand that everything's relative—

MICHELLE:

And you have to understand something, too ... You have to understand you're not alone in this world, and when you went away, you left six million people behind! That's what you don't want to understand, Ma! You took off when the house was on fire, and now you act as if the fire never happened! You were doubly happy to be discovered by your foreign conductor because we were going through a pretty

depressing period here, after the referendum, and
nothing much was happening, and your marriage was
falling apart and all the nationalists were turning into
whining cynics! If all the artists who thought like you
had left Québec after the 1980 referendum, we'd be
left with a bunch of international stars travelling
'round the world, is that it? Should everybody have
taken off and abandoned everything? Some people
didn't have the same opportunities as you, Ma!

PATRICIA:

I hope you're not referring to yourself, because you
did have the same opportunity! You could have taken
off from here whenever you wanted!

MICHELLE:

Yes, and when I had the choice, I chose to come back
here with my father, if you remember correctly! Not
everyone is meant for the life you lead!

PATRICIA:

I can't believe that's the only excuse you can find!

MICHELLE:

It's not an excuse. I've gone through all sorts of
periods, Ma, I've had all sorts of reactions, I've hated
you, all the people your age, for not delivering the
goods you promised, I've despised you for giving up
the way you did, blaming others instead of keeping
up the fight, or escaping the way you did. I even went
so far as to check out the other side of the fence,
overreacting, just because I was fed up, too, ten years
later, but ... if you have to choose one mess over
another, I prefer my own mess, the one I'm
responsible for myself and I don't have to be
ashamed, because even if I got stuck with it, it's
familiar. And what's familiar is the lesser of two evils
... because I'm not sure, I'm not sure, not sure I'm
capable of thinking for myself!

PATRICIA:

Ah, ha! You see, you admit the whole thing's a mess yourself!

MICHELLE:

Yes, Ma, everyone knows now that it's all a big mess, no matter which side you're on. We're not as innocent and naïve as you all were, and that's why it's important to go on.

Silence.

PATRICIA:

Nothing's worse than nostalgia. I listen to you talk, and I can hear myself thirty years ago … My god … It feels good to fight, doesn't it?

MICHELLE:

It's not too late, Ma.

PATRICIA:

Yes, it is too late. You know, even in those days, maybe it was too late, and the ones who got away are the only ones who can know that.

MICHELLE:

Ma, don't say that! You have no right to say that! You know it's not true.

PATRICIA:

If you only knew how much I believed in it. We thought it was only a question of time! We could feel it! It was the first time we'd ever dreamed of doing something *together*, you understand. We'd worked so hard, if you only knew! We'd come so far! We'd left so much behind, humiliation, intellectual mediocrity, all the little daily compromises that made us feel so ashamed! We thought, it's all over, finished, it will never happen again! We'll sweep it all away and start anew. And, who knows, maybe none of it was ever true! Maybe, when you get right down to it, we never even came close! We were kidding ourselves! Kidding ourselves! Pure self-delusion, that I spun with my own hands ... and it simply unravelled ...

The doorbell rings.

PATRICIA:

Saved by the doorbell! That must be your grandmother!

She heads for the intercom.

PATRICIA:

I'd completely forgotten about her in the heat of the action.

MICHELLE:

That's your speciality—

PATRICIA:

I wasn't even worried anymore. Mum, where have you been? Richard! What are you doing here?! I thought you lived in some dump up in Rosemont, or somewhere like that? Of course, come on up! It's penthouse #2, remember? Don't go to the other door, the guy who lives there is gay, we'll never see you again!

MICHELLE:

I'll take your suitcases into the bedroom.

She exits with the suitcases.

PATRICIA goes to open the door and stands in the door-way.

PATRICIA:

(loudly, as soon as the elevator door opens) My god! You've still got your grubby bag that looks like it's been through the war! Haven't you stopped by your place yet?

RICHARD appears, enters.

RICHARD:

> No, I had something else to do first ... Listen, I need to talk to you.

PATRICIA:

> Right now?

RICHARD:

> It's important ...

PATRICIA:

> In full jetlag? I've had my fill of important talks for today ... Sorry, but I'm tired ... Go home and take a nice shower, go to bed early, and call me in the morning. We're bound to wake up early anyway—

RICHARD:

> I'm sorry to insist ...

> *MICHELLE reenters.*

MICHELLE:

> Hello, Richard.

RICHARD:

> *(annoyed)* Oh, you're here, hello ...

> *They greet each other, with perfunctory kisses on each cheek.*

MICHELLE:

> Don't look so happy to see me!

RICHARD:

> It's just that I had some things to discuss with Madame Pasquetti ...

MICHELLE:

> Her name's Paquette around here, Richard.

PATRICIA:

> She just realized that her name isn't Paquette anywhere anymore, Michelle ...

> *The doorbell rings again.*

PATRICIA:
Good, this has to be her!

RICHARD frowns.

MICHELLE:
My grandmother.

RICHARD:
Shit!

PATRICIA:
(on the intercom) Mum! It's about time! I thought
you'd been kidnapped by a crowd of admirers ...
Come on up ... *(to RICHARD)* I'm sorry, Richard, but
it'll have to wait till tomorrow ...

RICHARD:
I can see that ...

PATRICIA goes to wait in the doorway.

MICHELLE:
Ma, how many times have I told you not to do that!

PATRICIA:
I'm too old to be kidnapped.

MICHELLE:
That's not what you just said to your mother. Anyway,
these days they're only interested in money! The
white slave trade went out of style in Montreal ages
ago!

PATRICIA:
I was just joking, Michelle. Relax!

*The minute she sees the elevator door open, PATRICIA
rushes to meet her mother.*

PATRICIA:
Oh, my dear sweet Mummy ...

MICHELLE rolls her eyes.

RICHARD:
Is she the same as ever?

MICHELLE:
Which one? Neither one of them has improved with age!

RICHARD:
I meant your grandmother, is she still as outspoken as ever?

MICHELLE:
(smiling) She'll be outspoken till the day she dies!

PATRICIA and ESTELLE enter.

ESTELLE is wearing a magnificent fur coat.

ESTELLE:
(laughing) Good lord! Michelle's here, too. I hope you're not going to splatter paint on this fur coat that cost me an arm and a leg!

She laughs heartily.

MICHELLE:
(to RICHARD, still smiling) Oops, ready, here we go!

PATRICIA:
God, you're looking gorgeous!

ESTELLE:
I was born looking gorgeous, my dear! And I specified in my will that I want to be buried in this coat! They can pluck out my eyes, if they want, and auction me off in little pieces, like in *Jesus of Montreal,* but they can't have my coat.

She laughs.

PATRICIA:
I hope it's paid for?

ESTELLE:
(without missing a beat) I'd like to remind you, dear, when I show up somewhere, I'm the one who gets the good lines.

PATRICIA:
I stopped doing supporting roles a long time ago, Mum.

ESTELLE:
Elsewhere, maybe, in the marvellous world of opera, in Munich, Berlin or Paris, but back here, you are still Estelle Bergeron's daughter, and you've got to act accordingly!

PATRICIA rolls her eyes, but pulls back.

ESTELLE:
Hey, is somebody going to offer to take my coat, or am I supposed stand here and drown in my sweat?

MICHELLE:
I'll take it for you, grandma ...

ESTELLE:
My god, you don't refuse to touch it?

MICHELLE:
I'm not sixteen anymore.

ESTELLE:
Okay, so I'll leave it to you in my will ...

MICHELLE is a bit taken aback.

ESTELLE:
Hah! Got you there, didn't I?

Grande dame, ESTELLE takes off her coat and settles into an armchair.

PATRICIA:
What's all this talk about wills, Mum? Did you finally write one?

ESTELLE:
I don't think you'd be interested in my inheritance, Patsy! If I divided everything I have between the two of you, you'd each end up with half of the mortgage

I've been renewing for the past thirty years, and half of a fur coat, also mortgaged to the hilt!

PATRICIA:
You love to cry poormouth, but I'm sure you've got more stashed away than you admit.

ESTELLE:
(as if she hadn't heard a thing) It smells stuffy in here.

PATRICIA:
Mum! Nobody's been living here for the past eight months!

ESTELLE:
I didn't say I don't know why, I'm just saying it smells stuffy in here. Open a window or a door, or something ... The St. Lawrence River flows by your penthouse, there's a great breeze outside, air the place out a bit ...

PATRICIA looks at MICHELLE who goes to open the door to the terrace.

ESTELLE:
I just found out yesterday that you were coming home ... Is this an impromptu vacation or are you running away from bad reviews like last time?

PATRICIA:
I've never run away from bad reviews!

ESTELLE:
You've got a lousy memory. Whenever your reviews are generally good, you send them to us by fax or by email and we're supposed to read them fast and call to congratulate you; when the reviews are generally bad, we see you show up here, with your tail between your legs and fit to be tied. *(to RICHARD, before her daughter can say a word)* Can't you sit down, Richard, I'm getting a crick in my neck.

RICHARD sits down in one of the other armchairs.

PATRICIA:
Richard was about to leave, Mum.

ESTELLE:
Richard will leave when I say he can leave! *(to RICHARD, mockingly)* Are you still tickling the ivories?

RICHARD:
(visibly intimidated) Of course. That's how I earn my living.

ESTELLE:
(indicating the duffel bag RICHARD has dragged along with him) Did you just accompany our great cantatrice in Europe somewhere?

RICHARD:
Yes. Yesterday. In Paris.

ESTELLE:
Did she call you at the last minute, as usual?

RICHARD glances toward PATRICIA.

ESTELLE:
I'm the one who's talking to you, Richard.

PATRICIA:
You can answer ...

RICHARD:
Well, yes, she did call quite recently.

ESTELLE:
When?

RICHARD:
The day before yesterday.

ESTELLE:
Does she make it worth your while, at least? She should, calling you at the last minute like that. She's famous for being tight-fisted ...

RICHARD:
I think I'm well paid for what I do.

PATRICIA:

He's very well paid for what he does.

She immediately regrets her words, but doesn't take them back.

ESTELLE:

(sharply, to her daughter) I hear you're still singing Salomé at your age! Nowhere but at the opera would they dare ... How old is Salomé supposed to be? Fourteen?

PATRICIA:

We know you've never liked opera, Mum.

ESTELLE:

Aren't you embarrassed? I don't know, but during the dance of the seven veils, aren't you afraid you'll scare Herod to death? *(she laughs heartily)* How come they let you opera singers get away with things they'd never tolerate from us actors?

PATRICIA:

(who's been through this scene hundreds of times) I've told you a thousand times, it's all about the voice and the music—

ESTELLE:

Bullshit! You're on stage, for god's sake, the least you could do is look vaguely like the character you're playing!

PATRICIA:

(about to lose her patience) The music is the most important thing ...

ESTELLE:

If the music is so important, why go to all the trouble of dressing up? Just give concert performances and sing your lungs out! If I had dared play Oscar Wilde's Salomé at your age, they'd still be talking about it, and with good reason! *(She laughs.)* I don't think anyone's dared since Sarah Bernhardt ... and

72

everybody knows that by the end of her career, it wasn't her people were going to see, it was her wooden leg!

MICHELLE can't help but smile.

ESTELLE:

(to MICHELLE) Your grandmother's still pretty quick with the repartee, don't you think?

MICHELLE:

You always were, Grandma!

ESTELLE:

(to PATRICIA) It reminds me of when you attempted to sing *The Barber of Seville* at the Montreal Opera four or five years ago ... You were about as funny as a stovepipe! You're meant to do comedy, like I'm meant to sing *The Flying Dutchman* ...

PATRICIA:

It was a beautiful production!

ESTELLE:

It was a grotesque production! There's nothing more excruciating than humour in opera! When it's dramatic, you all whip out your grand gestures and roll your eyes, and it can just about pass, but when you try to be funny! That time I felt like stomping onto the stage and giving you all a good slap! And that guy who was singing Bartolo, where in god's name did you dig him up?! C'mon, don't opera lovers ever go to the theatre? How can they split a gut laughing at something they'd never let an actor get away with in the theatre across the street? Do they check their brains with their coats? When it's bad, it's bad, for heaven's sake, whether it's spoken or sung!

PATRICIA:

Why are you dredging that up again? We've been talking about this for thirty years.

73

ESTELLE:

Would you believe I recently got sucked in again! I swore I'd never go back to the opera unless you were singing ... as long as it wasn't a comic role! Anyway. *(laughing)* Can you imagine a two-hundred pound Manon Lescaut? Well, I saw one, two months ago, and I'm still having nightmares.

PATRICIA:

Aww, Mummm ...

ESTELLE:

Okay, okay, I'll spare you the details ... But I'm telling you, when she was dying of thirst in the Louisiana desert at the end, she was holding enough water to keep herself and her beloved des Grieux alive for months!

RICHARD and MICHELLE laugh.

ESTELLE:

What does she sing? *Non voglio morir ...* She didn't want to die, she wanted to nurse her calf! *(Everyone laughs, even PATRICIA almost smiles.)* Besides, she could've been des Grieux's mother! Ah, that reminds me ... You know non-sequiturs are my speciality ... I've got some surprising news for you, Michelle ... Unless you've already heard ... *(to PATRICIA)* And you may as well find out right away, Salomé, while you're here in person. *(to MICHELLE)* Do you believe they've asked me to play your mother in your TV series? ...

PATRICIA and MICHELLE both react. ESTELLE bursts out laughing.

ESTELLE:

(to PATRICIA) We're erasing a generation! You no longer exist! You can disappear in Munich or Milan for the rest of your days.

MICHELLE:

Did you accept?

ESTELLE:

The director said you look a bit older than your age,
which is true … (*preening a bit*) And since I don't look
my age …

She laughs.

ESTELLE:

Exactly the reaction I expected … Two long faces!

RICHARD:

I really should be on my way …

ESTELLE:

Don't be silly, stay put and enjoy the show! You'll be
able to tell the story to … who knows, do you have a
psychiatrist? This is the kind of thing they love …

PATRICIA:

(*visibly upset*) Don't do that.

ESTELLE:

Do what?

PATRICIA:

Don't accept the role.

ESTELLE:

In case you've forgotten, my dear, I have to earn a
living! I'm not independently wealthy! Even though
you seem to think I am! I have to pay for this coat! It
wasn't a gift from a famous furrier so I could parade
around town, gushing its merits and virtues! Do you
remember how much we get paid in the theatre? The
price of one of your meals at Boffinger's where you
took me last year and I almost choked when I saw the
price of a side order of fries! So let me earn my living
with a little television role.

MICHELLE:

So you've signed the contract?

ESTELLE:

Not at all. I told the producer I wanted to talk to you
first. I wanted you to hear about it from me. I
certainly didn't want you to find out after the fact.
And I wanted your consent! Really. If it makes you
uncomfortable, if you want me to refuse the role, I'll
refuse it.

MICHELLE:

After what you just said—

ESTELLE:

Forget what I just said. I've never been short of work,
ever, you know that. I'll go play someone else's
mother, on some other show, to pay for that coat ...
But I want you to know that I feel like it ... I feel like
acting with you because I think you're good ...
because I'm proud of you ... because it would be fun,
it would be an honour, for me, to play opposite my
granddaughter.

PATRICIA:

Don't listen to her. She'll say anything to get her way.

ESTELLE:

It's true that I think she's good! Because I've seen
her perform. I've watched her grow since she was at
the theatre school ... Because I've gone out of my
way to see everything she's been in. Which is more
than you can say!

PATRICIA:

I almost came back to see her in the Espace Go
production at the beginning of the season—

MICHELLE:

(under her breath) Right, you *almost* came—

PATRICIA:

You two don't seem to realize that I sign contracts
years in advance, years in advance, and I can't always
do what I want!

MICHELLE:

(under her breath) That's not what you said a while ago.

PATRICIA:

I can't improvise my life from one day to the next,
like you two!

MICHELLE:

Do you really think we accept a role the day before
the show opens?

PATRICIA:

You know very well that's not what I meant ... But I
can't cancel something, just like that, at the last
minute and jump on a plane ... You don't have to
take a plane to visit each other.

MICHELLE:

But you cancel performances much more often now,
for the slightest cold, or the slightest "difference of
artistic opinion" between you and the director or the
conductor ... Like today, for instance, aren't you
supposed to be singing in *La Somnambula* in Milan?
Or Marseille? Isn't some singer trying to fit into one
of your costumes, as we speak?

ESTELLE:

You should learn how to improvise your life a bit
more ... If you really did sign that contract for *Salomé*
a few years ago, did you still feel like doing it? And if
you sign a contract now to do *Butterfly* in three years,
are you going to traipse around the stage at the
Opéra Bastille dressed up like a thirteen-year-old
Geisha when you're over fifty?

PATRICIA:

Stop talking about a world you don't know—

ESTELLE:

(cutting her off) And one I never want to know either!
A world where they make a travesty of theatre every
night—

PATRICIA:
Mum!

ESTELLE:
I'm saying what I think! And if you don't like it, you can go to your room! You opera singers live in an isolated world. You're out of touch with everything except what you do, because you never go to see anything else! And all you know how to do is make faces, wave your arms and hit pretty notes! Even when you get to work with great directors, you can't pull it off, because you're not interested! Do you want to hear more? You want me to lay it on? You know I can!

PATRICIA:
I know you can ... You've always been great at generalizing! You take one isolated case and you turn it into a generalization!

ESTELLE:
The operas I've seen were not isolated cases! But there's no sense in carrying on like this, we've never seen eye to eye on this subject and we never will.

PATRICIA:
Exactly.

ESTELLE looks at RICHARD.

ESTELLE:
You enjoying the show?

RICHARD wishes he could die.

MICHELLE:
It's true, there's no sense in carrying on—

ESTELLE:
You can say that again! There's nothing deafer than someone who doesn't want to hear!

PATRICIA shrugs her shoulders.

PATRICIA:

Well, I'm beginning to feel seriously tired.

ESTELLE:

We just got here! Nobody's even offered me a drink.

MICHELLE:

I bought some orange juice for Ma ...

ESTELLE:

You call that a drink? I don't drink anything that's good for my health, it makes me sick. Would you have a little vodka to liven up your orange juice?

PATRICIA:

You know there's no alcohol in this house.

ESTELLE:

And it's a real drag, too! Bring me a nice tall glass of water, Michelle. I don't dare ask if you have any Evian ...

MICHELLE:

You're in luck, we do!

> *MICHELLE exits.*

ESTELLE:

(laughingly) Good lord! Such extravagance! This is Babylon! Sodom and Gomorrah! Speaking of which, are you still living alone, Richard?

> *RICHARD reacts.*

ESTELLE:

Don't tell me you thought I didn't know! Do you think a straight guy would let my daughter walk all over him like this? He would have put her in her place ages ago!

PATRICIA:

Another one of her scathing judgements!

ESTELLE:

Something you're never guilty of, right? I'm sorry,
Richard, I didn't mean to embarrass you.

RICHARD:

That's all right ... Anyway, the answer is, yes, I'm still
living alone.

MICHELLE returns.

ESTELLE:

Mmmm, good to the very last drop.

She empties the glass.

ESTELLE:

If I wasn't afraid of getting tipsy and losing my license
for a year, I'd ask for seconds.

PATRICIA shrugs her shoulders. MICHELLE smiles.

MICHELLE:

I don't mind about the part, Grandma ...

ESTELLE:

(delighted) Really?

MICHELLE:

I'm sure it'll be great working with you.

ESTELLE:

It's always great working with me. I'm a real trooper!

*PATRICIA obviously feels excluded. ESTELLE looks at
her.*

ESTELLE:

Now what could I say to embarrass you?

PATRICIA:

Don't bother ... Let me get some rest. You can
embarrass me tomorrow.

ESTELLE:

No, I insist, I want to embarrass you today! Oh, right!
I almost forgot ... Would you believe I just refused
the Order of Canada! I received a lovely letter,

announcing the wonderful news, and I wrote them a lovely letter announcing that I refused the honour! You've received them all, if I remember correctly. The Order of Canada *and* l'Ordre du Québec? And Chevalier de l'Ordre des arts et des lettres de France, if I'm not mistaken. You see, Richard, that's what they call covering all your bases ... *(indicating PATRICIA)* Some people grab everything that comes their way ... *(indicating MICHELLE)* and others put all their eggs in one basket.

PATRICIA:

Do I detect a bit of jealousy?

ESTELLE:

Me, jealous! Are you crazy? Although ... If you're talking about your career, maybe I am. A career like yours is impressive. Yes, my dear, I admit that you impress me ... does that shut you up? An international career is an international career. When you left town with your little suitcase and your big ambitions, I thought you'd be back in no time, with your tail between your legs and your ambitions shattered, but you were courageous, you persevered, you struggled and you succeeded where few singers from here have succeeded, bravo, congratulations, I'm proud of you! It's true! Don't give me that look! Learn how to take a compliment!

PATRICIA:

Your compliments are so rare ... they're suspect.

ESTELLE:

You're drowning in compliments, Patsy, you're surrounded by your court of bootlickers who gush praise every time you sing a bar of vaguely difficult music. I can't believe you need my praise.

PATRICIA:

(softly) Of course, I do ...

ESTELLE:

Anyway, that's all great, but living out of suitcases and in hotel rooms like you do, even if the hotels are all four-star national monuments, no, thanks! Changing partners three times a week, dressing up like a teenage Geisha one night and a teenage Ethiopian girl three days later ... no. That's not for me. Offer me two years in the same show in London, New York or Paris, okay, any day ... Here our productions never run long enough! By the time we really get into a role, we've exhausted the audience for that show. But not knowing who I'll be working with the day after tomorrow ... or in what language ... or on what set, in what production ... Walking onto the stage without having rehearsed enough, and wondering which one of the perspiring fat men standing there is Rodolfo—

PATRICIA:

That's the exciting part, Mum ... It's different every time ... every performance is an adventure ... Your partner's singing style is different, his acting style is different ... you know his reactions will be different than the singer three nights ago ... and the character won't be exactly the same, even if the music remains identical ... Sometimes, all of your partners have changed and you have no idea what will happen! You find yourself on a set you've never seen before, but artists' digs are artists' digs, and the Mimi you'll sing that night will figure out how to feel at home, that's how it works.

ESTELLE:

I must enjoy routine more than you do—

PATRICIA:

You said it, not me ...

ESTELLE:

But doesn't it make you feel like you're always doing the same thing and always performing the roles in the same way because you never have time to work on them? Doesn't it feel like the same character in a different disguise? And don't you all feel like you're not performing together, that Rodolfo is still singing in the Munich production while you're singing in the one from Brussels?

PATRICIA:

That's what you don't understand, Mum. They don't come to see the actress perform, they come to hear the singer sing!

ESTELLE:

Maria Callas was both! Why shouldn't it always be both?

PATRICIA:

Not everybody has Maria Callas' talent.

ESTELLE:

She finally admits it!

PATRICIA:

I never denied it!

ESTELLE:

Sometimes when you talk about yourself, it sounds like Maria Callas was a minor satellite in a galaxy of stars where you are the supernova! My god, I have a way with words!

RICHARD smiles, delighted. PATRICIA is visibly exasperated, but she doesn't answer.

ESTELLE:

Do you still talk about yourself in the third person, or did you get over that? *(imitating her daughter in an interview)* "Yes, Patricia Pasquetti was performing in Saint Ying-Yang de Costa three days ago." Ridiculous! Kathleen Battle has more humility than that! And doesn't that business with the all medals and the political plums make you uncomfortable?

PATRICIA:

What political plums? There's nothing political about those awards,

ESTELLE:

Not in France, but what about here?

PATRICIA:

Not here either!

ESTELLE:

C'mon ... When they give them to you, you don't think it's because ... maybe ... they think you're on their side?

PATRICIA:

Not at all! It's in recognition of what ... what I am, what I've accomplished ...

ESTELLE:

I'd be embarrassed to accept them, if I were you ... I'd feel ... associated with them, obligated to them, and I'd be afraid they'd try to use me. And that goes for both sides. Those people never give anything for free. You scratch my back, I'll scratch yours. It's a vicious tit-for-tat game. When Québec gives you a medal, they expect you to stay on their side, even if you no longer live here, and it's the same thing in Ottawa, they do it so you'll change sides, or because they believe you already have!

PATRICIA:

You imagine things that don't exist ... It's called paranoia, Mum!

ESTELLE:

Well, I've always wanted to ... preserve my intellectual independence, and you know it. Even during, especially during, your big nationalist period. I've always steered away from politics. No matter which side. I don't think there's ever been a single picture of me with a member of any political party. On either side. I've always avoided it like the plague. I've never invited a minister to supper, and they've never laid eyes on me except on stage or on television ... So I've never been muzzled by my political opinions ...

MICHELLE:

But you have a responsibility to society, Grandma, as an artist—

ESTELLE:

My responsibility as an artist is to be good on stage. My political choices can be reflected in the roles I choose to play, but I refuse to appear on stage draped in a flag!

MICHELLE:

What if it can help change things, Grandma!

ESTELLE:

C'mon! Are people going to change their way of voting just because their favourite TV star leans one way more than the other!

MICHELLE:

Maybe, if we're convincing!

ESTELLE:

None of that has ever been proved. When they see me tackle a scene, they just see the actress, not a representative of a political party. Maybe if I was a popular singer ... If I were a popular singer, I'd know that I was singing for people who think like I do anyway, people already won over, and then maybe I'd take advantage of the situation ... but when I'm on stage, I'm there to play a character, to interpret a role, and if that role isn't politically coloured to begin with, I don't see why I'd add a layer that isn't there.

MICHELLE:

Everything is political, Grandma …

ESTELLE:

Especially the decision not to be political, I know,
you've told me that a hundred times. But this is a
free country, and I'm free to decide I don't agree! I
hope I have the right, that you haven't become a …
let's say the word, a fascist like your mother was when
she was young!

PATRICIA:

You used to call me a fascist, now you call me a
traitor!

ESTELLE:

Doesn't it come down to the same thing? Being sold
on one party or selling out to all of them, I don't see
the difference. I prefer to keep my opinions to
myself!

PATRICIA:

Ha!

ESTELLE:

We're talking about politics, Patricia!

PATRICIA:

I guess so, because it sure isn't true for *all other
subjects.*

ESTELLE:

(to MICHELLE) Your great-grandfather used to call
that being a free-thinker. It's been years since I've
heard that expression, because now it's not
acceptable. But I prefer to think that I'm like my
father who was proud to be a free-thinker! Such
freedom! That doesn't mean I don't have political
convictions, I do! And I've always voted! Always! And
for the right side, too! But you'll never know which
side! I'm not sold on any party, and I can remain
critical even of the ones I usually agree with! Because

86

the rest of the country doesn't know what I think! I've never belonged to anyone, so I don't see why I'd turn myself over to some political party. I have the reputation of being outspoken, but I refuse to speak out for only one side! I want the freedom to be outspoken about everyone, even the people I vote for!

MICHELLE:

You realize you're talking politics right now, and you're very convincing!

ESTELLE:

I'm with my family, with my daughter and granddaughter, and a musician who can hardly wait for me to leave so he can relax, because I terrify him! But I'd never have this conversation in public! And besides, I give you all permission to think whatever you want. You can even tell me to piss off, if you want, Michelle. I'm not trying to change your mind. I accept that you don't think like me, so accept that I don't think like you. I'm not saying I'm right, I'd never say that, but I have a right to think the way I do. I've never forced you to think anything, to be anything! Don't forget: free-thinker! That means thinking what you want, without imposing it on anybody else.

PATRICIA:

Go tell that to the taxi drivers you terrorize ...

ESTELLE:

I don't tell the taxi drivers what to think, I just tell them they don't know how to do their job!

PATRICIA:

You've spent your life telling people they don't know how to do their job. You're never satisfied with anything or anyone! You've become the terror of the taxi world because you've decided they don't know how to do their job. That's what you decided. Maybe you don't tell them what to think, but if you could take their place and show them how to work, you would!

ESTELLE:

You can say that again! Because I believe if something's worth doing, it's worth doing well. *(to MICHELLE)* Remain free! Don't feel obligated to follow anyone! And if you end up driving a taxi, make sure you don't let some crazy old lady tell you how to do your job … *(to PATRICIA)* You see, I even warn her against me! *(to MICHELLE)* But we can talk about all this when we're waiting around in the studio … And in the meantime, she's right, we should let your mother get some rest—before she kicks us out. She must be really tired, she hasn't answered me back. *(to PATRICIA)* The next time you sing *Butterfly*, Patricia, don't wear your Order of Canada medal, it's much too flashy!

She laughs and stands up.

ESTELLE:

Do you realize I didn't even give you a kiss when I came in? *(as she kisses her)* Welcome to Montreal, sweetie. I hope you didn't cancel a performance at the Berlin Opera to come kiss your old mother … I've got to go play a juicy role myself … in a little while I'll be on stage at the Rideau-Vert playing a Jewish mother from New York who's demonstrative and pushy, and believe me, I didn't have to do any research! And I don't have to perform the dance of the seven veils!

PATRICIA:

I wanted to have a real talk with you, but, you're right, I'm exhausted …

ESTELLE:

(gently) And I wanted to have a real talk with you, too.
But I arrived late as usual. I'm sorry. Listen, I don't
know why you've come home like this, unannounced,
but you never come back without a reason.

PATRICIA:

I felt like seeing you both—

ESTELLE:

Not really, Patricia, you never feel like seeing us.

PATRICIA:

That's not true.

ESTELLE:

Okay. You felt like seeing us. But when you feel like
seeing us, it's often after a flop, or after some bad
reviews—

PATRICIA:

I rarely have bad reviews!

ESTELLE:

And we don't see you often either ... Now, why did I
say that? Another flippant answer. Patricia, you've
been getting bad reviews more and more often in the
past few years, and you know it. We might pretend
not to know it, we might pretend not to read them,
but the European newspapers find their way here
sooner or later. The reviews you don't send us by fax
finally reach us anyway. You should move back home,
for good, before it's too late.

PATRICIA:

How can you say that, Mum! Move back here for
good! So I can be buried alive in the Montreal Opera
Chorus? And, too late for what?! It's not too late! For
anything! My career is going very well! That's your
jealousy speaking again!

ESTELLE:

I never got involved in your European career,
Patricia, because it was none of my business ... But
you're my daughter, I love you, and I don't want to
see you suffer ...

PATRICIA:

See me suffer! Did you hear that? See me suffer!

ESTELLE:

Patricia, you've always been spoiled, back here you've
always been treated like a great opera star, and in a
way, you are an opera star, but not great—

PATRICIA:

What are you trying to say?

ESTELLE:

You've always been ... let's say ... a commodity, in
Europe. It's true that you sing with Pavarotti, with
Domingo and Carreras, but you've never been a first
choice—

PATRICIA:

Wait, what game are you playing, I must be
dreaming—

ESTELLE:

(cutting her off sharply) We all know it, Patricia,
everybody knows it, but it doesn't matter. You pick up
roles in productions created by other singers, you are
a last minute replacement for sick singers, it's very
respectable, there's no shame in it, most of the
sopranos in Québec would kill their mother for that
experience. Let's say, you're a ... B list star. You never
made the A list, Patricia, even if you claim you did ...
You never had the top billing, and you never will!
Your name will always appear under the name of
your male partner because you never reached the
status of Callas or Sutherland or Tebaldi. Not even of

Scotto or Freni. Especially not now that ... that your
voice is really beginning to fail—

PATRICIA:

My voice is not beginning to fail!

ESTELLE:

You can deny it till the cows come home, but we have
ears. No matter how hard you try to disguise the
notes you can't hit anymore, and pass them off as
emotion, interpretation or an actress' whim, the
truth is you can't hit the damn notes anymore,
period! You have serious technical problems that are
going to catch up with you. You had a superb voice,
you've enjoyed a remarkable career, you've sung in
productions that will go down in opera history,
you've worked with Strehler, and Chéreau, and who
knows how many others, so come back now, before
it's too late! Or go hole up somewhere and work on
your voice, maybe there's still time. Others have done
it before you and it saved their lives. I'm not saying
this to humiliate you, Patricia, but for the past few
years I've been watching you sink into something that
could ruin your career over there, because you know
how cruel they can be, you've been living over there
long enough ... Stay here with us, work on your voice
before you go back ...

PATRICIA:

You're talking nonsense ...

ESTELLE:

I know you've never wanted to listen to my advice,
that you've always considered me a minor, local
celebrity, that you've even felt a bit embarrassed to
introduce me to Giorgio or Patrice ... but if I had
arrived earlier today, if I hadn't arrived late, would
what you told Michelle have changed anything about
what I just said? Tell me! Or would it have confirmed
all that? When I hear your voice on my answering

machine saying you'll be arriving on such and such a day, and when that day is not far off, I know something's wrong. I don't know why you've come back this time, but I do know, because it's always the case, I do know there has to be a reason. A negative reason!

MICHELLE:

If you give me permission to tell her everything you told me a while ago, Ma, I'll give her a lift. Anyway ...

PATRICIA:

(upset) Yes, do that, but choose your words ...

MICHELLE:

Don't worry, I never betray the author's words ... I'll report it exactly the way you told it ...

ESTELLE:

So, it's serious?

MICHELLE:

Yes, it's serious.

ESTELLE:

(to PATRICIA) Your recital the day before yesterday wasn't the triumph you claim it was? Is that it? The people you hoped to see there didn't show up? You took advantage of the fact you weren't wearing your glasses to pretend you didn't notice? You didn't come home because you were afraid of the reviews, you came home because you were afraid the newspapers wouldn't mention you, you were afraid there wouldn't be any reviews. That's why, isn't it? *(pause)* That's it.

PATRICIA doesn't respond.

ESTELLE looks to RICHARD for an answer.

He lowers his head.

Embarrassed silence.

MICHELLE:
(to RICHARD) I suppose you'd like a lift, too?

RICHARD:
Yes, thanks ... *(to PATRICIA)* I wanted to have a real
talk with you, too. But the situation didn't lend
itself—

PATRICIA:
Some other time, Richard. One bunch of insults is
enough for today ...

ESTELLE:
You shouldn't take what I said as insults, Patricia ...

PATRICIA:
I'm too exhausted to answer back now, Mum, but just
you wait—

> *RICHARD picks up his duffel bag and heads for the
> door. ESTELLE kisses her daughter again.*

ESTELLE:
I'm not asking you to answer me, Patricia, I'm asking
you to think about it ... Take care of yourself ... Get
some sleep. Sleep is the best escape. But tomorrow,
think seriously about what I said. Welcome home.
You'll always be welcome here.

PATRICIA:
I'd die here, Mum ...

ESTELLE:
You might die sooner, somewhere else ...

PATRICIA:
I'd rather get shot down in action, risking everything,
than just peter out, by playing safe. But you'll never
understand that!

> *ESTELLE stares at her daughter, not knowing what to
> say. MICHELLE kisses her mother goodbye.*

MICHELLE:
I'll call you tomorrow.

PATRICIA doesn't answer. RICHARD helps ESTELLE on
with her coat.

ESTELLE:

With an expensive coat like this ... I should wear a
plastic cover to protect it, like our mothers with their
living room sets ... and just take it off when I meet a
prime minister! *(She laughs.)* Bye!

PATRICIA:

Right, bye. And keep up the jokes.

> *The other three exit. PATRICIA rushes to the telephone*
> *and dials 411.*

PATRICIA:

(answering the recorded message) Montreal. No. Air
France, reservations ... *(she pushes a button, she glances*
at her watch, sighs, then, in her prissy accent) Hello! This
is Patricia Pasquetti, the cantatrice. I was on your
Flight 033 from Paris this afternoon ... No, I didn't
leave anything on the plane, but ... you might find
this a bit eccentric, you know how eccentric opera
singers can be ... I'd like to know if there are any
seats left on Flight 031 tonight ... yes, I did say
tonight ... if it's not too late, of course. *(delighted)* It's
been delayed? Really? Till what time? Fantastic! That
gives me just enough time to jump into a taxi. Yes,
that's right, it's a one-way return, no, no, money isn't
a problem, I'll arrange all that at the airport ...
Perfect, goodbye!

> *She hangs up, goes into her bedroom, then reappears*
> *with her suitcases. She sets them down, slips into her*
> *coat. She walks over to the door slowly, then opens it.*
> *She turns back, looks around her apartment, before*
> *returning to pick up her suitcases.*

PATRICIA:

Let them all go to hell, pathetic bunch of nobodies.

She exits.

RICHARD comes running into his psychiatrist's office, throws his bag under the piano, and sits down on the bench.

RICHARD:

I'm sorry to impose like this, between two appointments, but it'll only take a minute ... I'm so relieved! I didn't manage to talk to her, but her mother did it for me! And now I know how to shut her up! I just have to bark louder than her. When you bark louder than her, she cowers like a little puppy dog! You should've seen her. She just stood there, without saying a word. Now I know what to do in the future! I'll be like Herod at the end of *Salomé* when he shouts to the guards: "Get rid of this plague for me," and the guards crush Salomé beneath their shields. Now I can crush her whenever I want, thanks to the marvellous Estelle Bergeron who showed me how.

VOICE OF HEROD:

(in German) Man töte dieses Weib!

Strauss' Salomé theme is heard twice, and each time, Richard shouts:

RICHARD:

Yes! Yes!

The guards crush Salomé beneath their shields.

THE END

AGMV Marquis

MEMBER OF SCABRINI MEDIA

Quebec, Canada
2002